World's Ugliest DOGS

Vicki DeArmon

LP

LYONS PRESS
Guilford, Connecticut
An imprint of Globe Pequot Press

To buy books in quantity for corporate use
or incentives, call **(800) 962-0973**
or e-mail **premiums@GlobePequot.com.**

Lyons Press is an imprint of Globe Pequot Press.

Project editor: Lauren Brancato
Layout: Melissa Evarts
Text design: Sheryl P. Kober

Library of Congress Cataloging-in-Publication Data is available on file.

ISBN 978-0-7627-9255-9

Printed in the United States of America

10 9 8 7 6 5 4 3 2 1

For the dogs, of course!

THE World's **ugliest dog**®

Petaluma, California

C O N T E S T

The Question of Ugly

The World's Ugliest Dog® Contest is an unbridled celebration of all that is fantastically dog. And ridiculously funny.

Because dogs are funny by nature and ugly dogs are funnier still. It's a human truth, one that the World's Ugliest Dog Contest capitalizes on every year with the event that takes place during the annual Sonoma-Marin Fair in Petaluma, California.

This book is about these beautifully ugly dogs.

To enjoy it, you have to love dogs. And you have to have a sense of humor.

To me these things go together. Dogs and humor.

Dogs to me are smile igniters. They are intrinsically funny. They are as close to being people as animals get. They are the furry Mini-Mes of our society, reflecting back all that we put out there in the world.

Thank goodness they can't talk. We get to translate and put words in their mouths, something our other family members seem to reject on principle. A dog cocks his head and questions you over his long nose. "How was your day?"(Some might misconstrue that to mean, "Do you have a treat for me in your pocket?" but let's not mess with an owner's translation.) My dog often looks at me, for instance, and her eyes positively scream, "You are so fabulous I can hardly stand it. I think I'll whip around three times in a circle at your feet to prove it." Why can't my husband do that? She might rest her head on her paws and look up expectantly. "Okay, alpha leader, lead me." Why can't my children do that?

The World's Ugliest Dog Contest celebrates all that is fantastically dog. To enjoy it, you have to love dogs and you have to have a sense of humor.

Ugly dogs bring laughter to millions of people around the world.

Sometimes I catch my dog smiling at me, her leathery lips turning up capital C's in the corners, and I know she gets me. A wet nuzzle to the neck and I'm feeling I just might make it through a grim work week. My dog takes all the weight out of a heavy world.

That's what the ugly dogs of the World's Ugliest Dog Contest do too. They lighten the load for all of us in a world overburdened with heaviness. And that is why the photo of the winner always careens around the world, hitting thousands of media outlets and bringing laughter to millions of people.

And what do the dogs think about all this? Do their feelings get hurt when the "ugly" word is cast their way? To answer this specific question, last year we brought in the renowned pet psychic Sonya Fitzpatrick to host the contest. We wanted to discover, once and for all, what the dogs *were* thinking as they assumed the stage amid the thundering applause and hyperintensive shouting from the assembled fans. Were they humiliated? Ashamed? Did they turn their doggy noses down and wish they were at home gnawing privately on a bone? (And if so, why were their tails wagging so fiercely?)

Our psychic read each dog's psyche as he or she ascended the stage. Turns out they were mostly thinking of chicken strips—fried—the

Dogs offended by the word ugly? Certainly not, says the psychic.

smell wafting over the stage from the adjacent stand in a most persistent manner. Also, they were pondering where their next nap was coming from. Thank you, Sonya, for putting the notion that dogs are offended to rest. That should put an end to humorless e-mails sent by the one or two protesters who have never attended the contest and fervently believe it's just plain mean to associate dogs with the word "ugly."

The fact is that there are no ugly dogs. They may be "beauty challenged" or "unique," but if you ask their owners, these dogs are adorable. To the audience, the phrase most commonly used is "so ugly, they're cute."

Humans tend to love underdogs and ugly dogs define underdog (some of them do come adorned with capes). It's a contest specifically for underdogs, actually. These are dogs who are aesthetically challenged but also who have had some deep holes to dig before their fifteen minutes of fame arrived.

Many of the dogs entered in the World's Ugliest Dog Contest are shelter or rescue dogs. They are dogs who have been rescued from some pretty bad circumstances and brought home to a loving family. Their stories are in this book. And each time one of these dogs wins the title, the contest becomes more of a showcase event for loving and adopting shelter animals. That the dogs in the contest go on to be ambassadors of goodwill, encouraging people around the world to adopt animals from local shelters, is one of the best parts of the event.

There's no such thing as an ugly dog. Their owners think they are adorable. The fans say, "So ugly, they're cute."

So here's what's especially noble about the ugly dogs who come to the World's Ugliest Dog Contest. They are willing to dress in silly outfits and parade around on stage in front of thousands of dog lovers. This is a testament to their commitment to the service agreements dogs signed thousands of years ago when they first lay down beside humans to keep us warm. Given that we mostly all have shelter now in our advanced society, lying down beside us metaphorically means wearing silly outfits and subjecting themselves to the overzealous displays of affection inflicted on them by their owners. Despite what has happened to them, they are grateful to be loved. And the crowds? The cameras? The hoopla? They don't seem to mind the attention one bit.

Live from Petaluma

 The first thing that you should know is that the World's Ugliest Dog Contest is as "down home" as a contest can get, originating out of Petaluma, a small town in Northern California during its annual five-day fair. The Sonoma-Marin Fair is a small country fair unencumbered by sophistication. It is the best kind of fair, with corn dogs, funnel cakes, clickety-clacking rides full of screaming teens, exhibits in six buildings, all showcasing local wine, food, crafts, art, and livestock in the hot summer month of June. The annual World's Ugliest Dog Contest takes place on an outdoor stage in mid-fair with a dedicated audience of rabid dog lovers, many of whom stake out their bench under the giant awning a few hours in advance.

The point is that it ain't Madison Square Garden or the Westminster Kennel Club. In fact, the World's Ugliest Dog Contest is the anti-beauty contest. There's nothing elite about it. No preliminaries. You can pretty much load up your dog and drive in from Modesto that day if you want to enter. The only cost is the gas or airfare to the San Francisco Bay area.

But many people make their plans to attend many months out. It usually starts with an e-mail to the fair that includes a photo. I take a look at the photo, scream appropriately, e-mail back that I think they have a contender, and get them registered. Registering is free (unless you wait until the day of the contest).

And for the record, the total budget for producing this contest is about $500. That doesn't include the trophies and the prize money, which for all the categories of winners including the grand prize

winner amounts to $1,850. But seriously, could *American Idol* run their operation on such a minuscule budget? We can and we do. Occasionally we've garnered some sponsorship money, but not much, and every year I'm still scouting for set donations. A few years back, one of the contestants asserted we had gone Hollywood and were in it for the money. She was eyeing the documentary filmmakers and assumed that money was flowing our way. Uh, no. What part of "documentary" do you not understand?

The reason the Sonoma-Marin Fair holds the contest each year is to entertain its fairgoers. That it has swept the globe has been totally unexpected. There's been talk of selling the licensing and merchandising rights and making a mint (we use the same conversational tone that you assume when buying a lottery ticket), but really, it just never happens. And really, is there a mint to make? We're just too busy throwing the annual Sonoma-Marin Fair in Petaluma and having a good time.

The Sonoma-Marin Fair is a "down home" country fair that takes place in Petaluma, California, in the hot summer month of June. It has rides, funnel cake–eating contests, livestock and exhibits, and good old-fashioned corn dogs, and is also home to the world-renowned World's Ugliest Dog Contest.

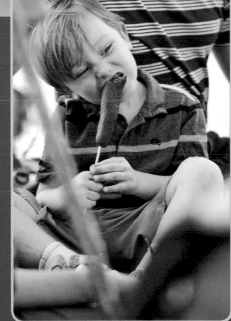

What Makes an Ugly Dog

The World's Ugliest Dog Contest judging criteria is based on four categories:

- First Impression
- Special or Unusual Attributes
- Personality
- Audience Impression

The First Impression is the horror or humor factor. The judges have to regulate themselves. Do they draw back in horror? Is it impossible to suppress a laugh? Is it indeed a dog? These are all questions they might ask themselves.

Then they look for special or unusual attributes such as:

- Droopy or crooked tail
- Strange or sad-sack eyes
- Cauliflower ears
- Unruly, odd color, or nonexistent coat

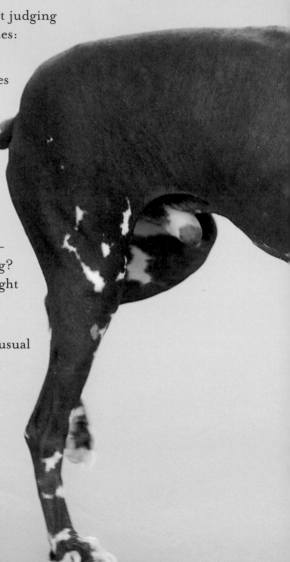

- Swayback
- Legs of different length
- Jutting jaw, severe underbite, or buck teeth

That said, personality is usually the big factor in winning the contest. Does the dog strut across the stage? Look off into the distance bored? Sigh majestically? Sport an amazing outfit? That's what influences the audience, and if the audience gets behind a dog, deafening cheering results, and the title is usually within reach. The audience definitely holds sway over the judges.

The World Loves an Ugly Dog

The world loves the ugly-dog celebration that is the World's Ugliest Dog Contest. How much do people love it? The announcement of the 2008 winner was rated by Yahoo as the third top story in the world (the first being the news of Michael Jackson's death and the second, an Obama speech at the height of his popularity). The website featuring the dog contestant photos catapulted to the top 100,000 sites in the world before the June event. And, in the weeks leading into the contest, *People* magazine, *The Today Show,* and the Huffington Post (to name a few) all have called looking for the story and the photos. Every year,

This is a contest that hollers out fun.

the image of the winner travels around the world, appearing in newspapers and evening broadcasts from Beijing to Brazil as well as hitting every city in the United States.

This is the appeal for media and fans, the grandiosity of a ridiculous contest. It hollers out fun. Ugly mugs transform formerly obscure dogs into stars each June while thousands of fairgoers watch and applaud and hundreds of media venues document every beauty-challenged snout and misaligned hair. With dogs as the celebrities, how can you miss?

Knockoff ugly-dog contests now pop up at every dog park fundraiser in America, but the World's Ugliest Dog Contest in Petaluma remains the granddaddy of them all—and everyone in the world of ugly dogs knows it. To win the trophy and title here is to be the World's Ugliest Dog, and the cachet that comes with that is no small thing. The prize from the fair—$1,000 and an enormous trophy—is wonderful, but there's far more value in the fame. The winning dog and owner will most likely be flown to New York for a spot on *The Today Show*. Johnny Carson, Jay Leno, and Carson Daly have interviewed the winners. The dog's photo appears in newspapers and on television programs around the world. This canine becomes a hero in his or her hometown and will be recognized on the street. The town's mayor may issue a proclamation. Local events in need of a celebrity now have one. Kids in school will have assemblies where the winning dog will be a demonstration of the principle "it's okay to be different." You get the idea.

The image of the winner travels around the world from Beijing to Brazil.

Media capture every beauty-challenged snout and misaligned hair.

Pedigreed dogs and mutts compete in the World's Ugliest Dog Contest.

The Dogs & Their Owners

Ugly dogs are a variety of breeds and mutts. The Chinese crested has been a dominant breed among the recent winners and has grown in popularity as a pet because of the contest. Because it's hairless, the Chinese crested has the distinct advantage of revealing what's under all that fur most dogs are cloaked in. It's usually a landscape of patterned skin, bumps, and irregularity, with occasional sprouts of hair. Additionally, they have few teeth and their tongues protrude, hanging like a permanent fixture to the side of their mouths like a bad attitude. Other breeds that appear frequently are bulldogs, pugs, Chihuahuas, and shar-peis—probably because so many of the special traits or attributes sought by the judges go with the breeds: overbites, underbites, bulging eyes, excess skin.

Where it goes off-road is with the Mutt class. There have been times when it's been unclear whether it even was a dog competing, so odd was the configuration of traits and attributes. At the contest, especially with the Mutt category, sounds (snuffling for instance) and walks (strolls, hops, butt scoots) add to the humor.

We have two kinds of contestants, the returning and the new. The new come because someone has told them, "My goodness that's an ugly dog." The returning come back because it's a blast and at this point, we're all one ugly-dog family. Most enter the contest just for fun. But others are on a quest for glory. Some of our more exuberant dog owners—worse than any beauty pageant mother—reveal their own quests for fame in their signs, T-shirts, and assembled groupies. These are the ones who have been bitten by the urge to walk the red

carpet through the throngs, dog held high above their heads, to try to claim the title of the World's Ugliest Dog, and they are serious about it. In the weeks before the contest, sniffing out the competition, making backstabbing comments, and seeing who can lift a leg higher around the hydrant of publicity become the dog owner's mission.

They come from all over the United States to compete: Florida, New Jersey, Pennsylvania, Tennessee, Colorado, Oregon, Idaho, and towns all over California. We've had interest from Brazil and Canada, but as yet only the United Kingdom has sent a representative. So yes, it's the World's Ugliest Dog Contest much the same as the World Series is still the World Series, with the difference being competitors from outside the United States are welcome.

We're all part of the ugly-dog family.

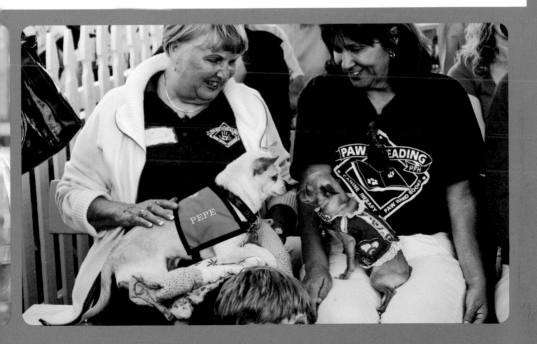

These dogs are well loved. In fact, many of our owners have made their lives revolve around their dogs. Where you find one, you'll find the other. It's hard to imagine Dane Andrew without Rascal by his side, for instance. For better or worse, the dogs and their owners may even have a faint resemblance to one another! But regardless, their person-alities are often intertwined and indistinguishable. There are Dane and Rascal, Kathleen and Princess Abby, Jon and Icky, perfect pairings of

Dogs (and owners) come from across the country, big personalities in tow.

animal and human, all of whom you're about to meet. The dog is in the forefront as the star, but the owner is there every step of the way, a stage mother of sorts, providing the backup rhythm to the dog's lead vocal.

Names like Handsome Hector, Spam-o-Rama, Icky, Rue, Creature, Princess Abby, Elwood, Pabst, Yoda, Archie, Rascal, and Mugly tell the story. These are dogs (and owners) with big personalities.

Nana & Yvonne Morones
(1996, 1997, 1998, 1999, 2000, 2001)

Nana, a tiny mutt weighing three pounds with curly black hair, a pink tongue and one good eye, rose to stardom through a six-year reign as champion. Animal lover Yvonne Morones found her in a kennel and fell immediately in love when Nana threw herself from the cage into Yvonne's arms. After that they were inseparable. After her victory at the World's Ugliest Dog Contest, Nana and Yvonne appeared on *The Tonight Show* with Jay Leno. The segment was so popular that Jay created his own ugly-dog contest. Nana was invited back for that and became the only dog in the history of the contest to be on Leno twice. On the show, she walked her trademark walk, which means she sidled along sideways like John Wayne in a Western or as if her dog biscuits had been spiked. It's part of what won her the title at the contest as well.

Nana rose to stardom with six con-
secutive title wins. She was the only
one to rival Chi Chi, who won eight
world titles. After Nana's passing,
her owner Yvonne Morones later
returned with Munchkin, a beloved
animal of indeterminate breed who
may well have been the reincarnation
of Nana.

Bob Weir of the Grateful Dead used a photo of Nana to illustrate the cover of an album for his band RatDog. Film crews from Japan, *Evening Magazine,* and Animal Planet all caught Nana in action as the celebrity dog she was as she visited the vet and the beauty salon. With her "pupperazzi," her star status was sealed.

Munchkin carried on the legacy with an appearance on *Last Call with Carson Daly,* and received the VIP treatment, complete with fans!

Rascal & Dane Andrew
(2002)

After winning the 2002 World's Ugliest Dog Contest, Dane Andrew and his dog Rascal, also a Chinese crested (Dane calls him a chupacabra or African sand dog), now compete each year in the Ring of Champions portion of the show. Dane himself has competed nonstop in the contest since 1977, when he was eleven years old.

They both have a long history with the contest. Rascal is ugly-dog royalty, being fourth in a dynasty that has held the coveted world title. Dane and his family first entered their rescue dog, Chi Chi, who is now in *Guinness World Records* for winning eight world titles. Rascal's grandmother, a rescue dog named Lady Pink, won the title three times. Lady Pink and Chi Chi had Mai Tai, who won another three titles, and then the son of Mai Tai, Rascal, claimed the title in 2002.

Rascal, who sports his patented trademark hot dog leash, is so unusual that Jay Leno put him on *The Tonight Show* before he even competed in the contest. Since then, Dane and Rascal have appeared in numerous national and international television shows, and Rascal has appeared in several horror films. Celebrity fans range from Pam Anderson to Adam West, who named Rascal the "Official Bat Dog."

Rascal and Dane travel with hot dog leash and sign for contests.
When not competing, Rascal has a busy acting career in horror films.

Sam & Susie Lockheed
(2003, 2004, 2005)

Over the course of the last twenty-five years of ugly-dog mania, one dog in particular has galvanized the world. Sam took the title for three straight years before his death at age fifteen; canonization on the Internet has made him one of the most beloved dead dogs in the world.

As much as you never want to say a dog is truly ugly, Sam was. He was a dog with no fur, an assortment of bumps riddled his skin, his eyes were rheumy, he sported the classic missing teeth and lolling tongue of the Chinese crested, and photos managed to capture a snarl that said, "Back off, Jack." Yet Sam was also the most revered of dogs. His owner Susie Lockheed of Santa Barbara took in Sam as a temporary rescue dog and fell in love. She brought him to the contest where he easily claimed the title and opened the door for other Chinese cresteds. She set up a website in honor of Sam upon his death and received six million views in a single day.

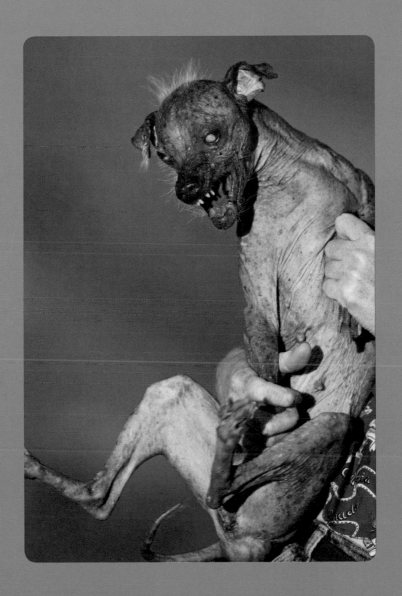

Since then the breed has grown in popularity and is one of the dominant breeds in the contest. Sam's picture often graces the stage at the annual contest to show what is possible when ugly is unleashed.

Sam defined the word ugly and took the title three years in a row. During his reign his website garnered more than 160 million hits and Sam was dubbed "the ugliest dog ever," according to his owner Susie Lockheed. His girlfriend Tater Tot (pictured below) may have been too cute to claim the title, said Susie.

Archie & Heather Peoples
(2006)

The official winner in 2006, Archie was selected by a panel of judges on June 23, in the first of three contests filmed by Animal Planet. Owner Heather Peoples maximized the Archie effect when she carried him up on her shoulder, his underbelly exposed in all its glory. The packed crowd went wild. Described by his owner as a "hairless sausage," Archie was thicker around the middle than the other Chinese cresteds

Described as a "hairless sausage" by his owner, Archie claimed victory in the Ring of Champions round of the contest.

and his skin—seriously bumpy terrain. Despite the stiff competition from an Italian greyhound named Victoria and a Chinese crested from Florida named Lucille Bald, Archie took the Pedigree class and then beat the winner of the Mutt class, Pee Wee Martini, who had just trumped Elwood and Tater Tot. The trophy—due to the presence

of Animal Planet—had grown to a six-footer and was a challenge to stuff in the car and take back to Arizona. Heather continues to make the pilgrimage to the contest each year, and when Archie died in a dog fight in 2008, she brought her dogs Reggie and Veronica, both Mexican hairless mixes. Reggie, with his irregular spurts of fur along the ridgeline of his back, made a run for the title a few times, placing but as yet not winning.

A longtime contestant and member of the ugly-dog family, Heather returns just for the fun of it with her Mexican hairless dogs Reggie and Veronica.

Elwood & Karen Quigley
(2007)

A Chinese crested/Chihuahua mix, Elwood won the title in 2007 with his distinct looks. His bug eyes, Mohawk, and dangling tongue evoked ET. The audience adored him.

Karen Quigley fell in love with this rescue dog from the local SPCA as soon as she saw him. Elwood came to live with her and a tribe of other rescue dogs in her home in New Jersey. He made an

Elwood retired from his ambassador duties just this last year, but not before raising hundreds of thousands of dollars for rescue groups and nonprofit animal organizations.

appearance in the 2006 contest, placing second in the Mutt class, and then returned to claim the title in 2007. Perhaps more than any other winner in the history of the World's Ugliest Dog Contest, Karen and Elwood have given back. After his victory, Karen and Elwood became ambassadors for rescue dogs everywhere, including *The View* with Barbara Walters in a segment about adopting rescue dogs. After Karen published a children's book, *Everyone Loves Elwood,* with the message that it's okay to be different, Elwood hit the school circuit spreading the love as well. Karen announced Elwood's retirement from his duties as an ambassador for rescue animals everywhere this last year, but only after his appearance at more than two hundred events, raising hundreds of thousands of dollars for rescue groups and nonprofit animal organizations.

Gus & Jeanenne Teed
(2008)

Gustopher Von Hausen Mausen (aka Gus) traveled from Florida with his owners, mother and daughter Jeanenne and Janey Teed, to capture the 2008 title. A Chinese crested, he was missing an eye (lost in a battle with a tomcat), and was suffering from cancer, which had already cost him his leg. Jeanenne had Gus for eight years prior to his cancer diagnosis and had rescued him from a crate in someone's garage.

Gus won the crowd over early on and by the time he got to the Ring of Champions round, where he met Archie, Elwood, and Rascal, he had the full support of the vocal audience and was crowned champion. This was the second event filmed by Animal Planet and this time hosting duties were shared by animal lover and activist Beth Ostrosky, who saw the beauty in each of the dogs and their stories.

However, a dog with one eye, three legs, and cancer was not really the kind of dog that could bring a smile to your face when given the title "ugly," even if the prize money was going to pay for cancer treatment. So the next year the fair introduced new contest rules requiring pre-contest vet checks. The dog must be "naturally ugly," rather than conditionally ugly due to health issues.

Gus's sad story won over the audience at the contest in 2008, but also initiated a change in the contest rules. In order for dogs to compete, they had to be "naturally ugly."

Pabst & Miles Egstad
(2009)

After seven years of Chinese crested wins, Pabst appeared as a fresh new face at the 2009 contest when his unassuming owner Miles Egstad drove down on a fluke from Citrus Heights, California. Pabst had a lot going for him. He had a fabulous name—given to him because he had a "bitter-beer face." And he was a boxer mix with a severe underbite and a sweet personality. I can still hear the crowd roaring "PABST, PABST, PABST!"

Pabst with his "bitter-beer" face had the personality of a champion and won over the judges and the audience quickly. He's pictured here with Karen "Doc" Halligan at the judges' table before his pronouncement in 2009 as the World's Ugliest Dog.

Miles was absolutely stunned by the victory and the level of attention. "I don't think he's that ugly," he said. A crew from Animal Planet taped this show for *Dogs 101*. This was the first year that the winner would also be awarded a $1,000 modeling contract and bling from House Of Dog, one of that year's contest sponsors. He also won a professional photo shoot with the official World's Ugliest Dog photographer Grace Chon. The following year, as part of his reign, Pabst participated in the fair's float at the Butter & Egg Day Parade in Petaluma, famously vacating his bowels—completely nonplussed—before a crowd of one hundred thousand. In the Sacramento area, Pabst and Miles helped at dog rescue rallies. Ultimately though, Pabst retired early, preferring chewing on bones and chasing sticks to the annual competition.

Princess Abby
& Kathleen Francis
(2010)

Just as most competition shows roll out the backstory of their contestants, at the World's Ugliest Dog Contest, the backstory often provides the pivotal moment in deciding who is going to win the contest. The dog has to command attention, but the story gets the audience's favor.

It's a Cinderella "tail." Princess Abby's charmed life began when she met Kathleen and went on to win the 2010 World's Ugliest Dog title. Now she returns each year to compete in the Ring of Champions.

Princess Abby is a one-eyed dog whose hind legs are nearly half again as long as her front. Princess Abby and her owner Kathleen Francis both came to the contest with compelling stories. A rescue dog of indeterminate breed, Princess Abby was the product of a puppy mill and inbreeding before Kathleen took her home from the pound. Kathleen herself had just suffered the death of her senior partner and was in financial crisis. On a whim and at the suggestion of friends, Kathleen came to the contest—and won. Kathleen has always said (as many of the owners do) that Princess Abby was as much a gift to her life as she was to Abby's. Following the contest, that had even more truth when her unfinished home was completed by volunteers who wanted to do something special for Abby. In her hometown of Clearlake, California, both she and Princess Abby are celebrities. The town authorities even issued a proclamation honoring Princess Abby, and she's called to appear at events from Sacramento to Oakland.

Yoda & Terry Schumacher
(2011)

Dog or rat? Many times it's been unclear if in fact these are actual dogs competing, especially in the Mutt class. Yoda from Hanford, California, won the title of World's Ugliest Dog 2011, but fourteen years earlier even his owner, Terry Devine Schumacher, was unsure of his species. She reportedly told her two-year-old daughter, who had found him in a field, to "put it down" because she thought Yoda was a rat. After closer inspection they learned otherwise and Yoda joined the family.

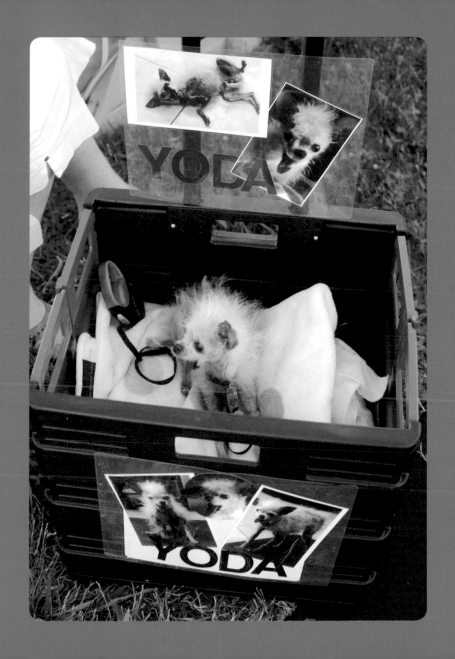

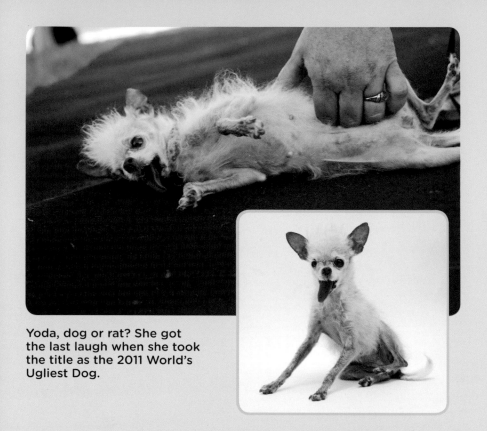

Yoda, dog or rat? She got the last laugh when she took the title as the 2011 World's Ugliest Dog.

Years later, Yoda took the title at the Sonoma–Marin Fair where her irregular features, scruffy fur, and tiny size of 1.8 pounds made her a crowd favorite, beating out candidates such as Icky, Cuda, Handsome Hector, Ratdog, and a field of twenty-five other contestants of questionable beauty. The trophy was fifteen times her size. Yoda also won a photo shoot with the year's official photographer, Kira Stackhouse of Nuena Photography.

WORLD'S UGLIEST DOG® 2011
Sonoma-Marin Fair, Petaluma

Mugly & Bev Nicholson
(2012)

In 2012, Bev Nicholson and her dog Mugly arrived from the United Kingdom to claim the title. A Chinese crested, Mugly was the unofficial ugly dog of the UK, with many press clips already amassed. His entourage included a British film crew, intent on documenting Bev and Mugly's every move for the television show *Dead or Alive*. To celebrate our first international contestant, the fair held a press conference

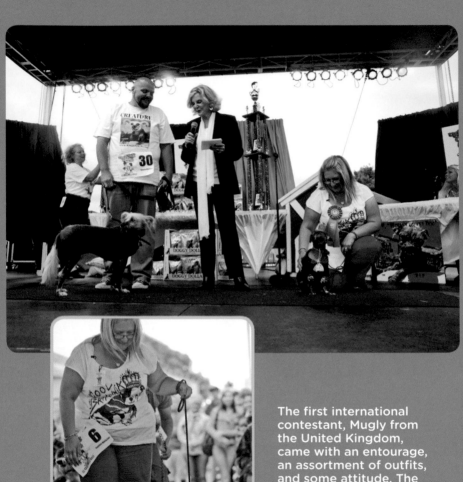

The first international contestant, Mugly from the United Kingdom, came with an entourage, an assortment of outfits, and some attitude. The title in 2012 was his.

at the San Francisco SPCA in what was billed as a Doggie Throw-Down. Representing the United States: Jon Adler and Icky. Representing the UK: Bev and Mugly. Flags were waved, speeches made, tails wagged. And of course, the media came.

The introduction of a contestant from outside the United States made the contest truly worldwide. At the contest itself, it made Mugly's victory almost inevitable, despite tough competition from a dog named Creature who had traveled with his owner Taylor Stokes from Utah. Creature, a Mexican hairless, had ears that stood at attention and a substantial underbite. The audience weighed in for both. But Mugly, resplendent in an outfit that sold his talents, soared through each stage of the contest with gaining momentum until he took the title and was whisked away in a limo to the Sheraton Sonoma County for a special dinner and dog-friendly overnight stay. How they got the trophy home to the UK is still a mystery!

Other Notable Mugs

Over the years, I've had the opportunity to meet some great dogs and their owners. For a variety of reasons, they did not win the grand title of World's Ugliest Dog, but for reasons of looks and personality, I feel they nonetheless deserve mention here. I'm sure there were many dogs before my tenure as well!

One such entry is Jon Adler and his dog Icky, who hail from Chico, California. Jon has been the unofficial contest cheerleader, stirring it up and keeping other contestants looped in on his Facebook page. Jon's spiked Mohawk matches Icky's, though Icky of course does not have the tattoos. Icky often places in the contest but somehow never takes the title, but the good news for Jon and fans is that he is young and therefore he has a long life ahead in which he can only get uglier.

Each year, the contest has multiple winners before the final winner is declared.

Jon Adler, pictured here with Icky, is the unofficial contest cheerleader.

Miss Ellie, owned by Dawn Goehring, won the Pedigree class, but not the title.

There's a winner for the Pedigree class and a winner for the Mutt class. Those two have a runoff for the ugliest dog of the year and then that dog takes on past winners in the Ring of Champions. That final round is what determines the World's Ugliest Dog. But the point is there are lots of ways to claim ugly-dog status and because of that, it can get confusing about who won what. Miss Ellie won the Ugliest Dog of the Pedigree class in 2009, but not the ultimate title. Yet when Miss Ellie passed away in 2010, news headlines proclaimed, "World's Ugliest Dog Dies," even though the actual winning dog lived on in Pabst. To repeat, Miss Ellie did not win the title of World's Ugliest Dog. But Miss Ellie, owned by Dawn Goehring from Tennessee, was notable just the same. A Chinese crested, she had only a couple of teeth, and moles and pimples with sporadic patches of hair covered her skin. And then there was the bow atop her head.

Another favorite of mine was Munchkin, a past contender owned by Yvonne Morones, who also was the owner of the six-time winner Nana. Munchkin defied all species affiliation. Truly there was only one of these dogs made and Munchkin was it. A wide grin across her face, a snuffling sound as she shuffled across the stage, her hair in a Phyllis Diller send-up . . . we all wondered, what was she? A short Snuffleupagus? Yvonne called her a "canardly," as in you "can hardly" tell what she is. After winning the honor of the year's ugliest dog in 2005, she went up against Sam in the Ring of Champions. Sam was one of the few dogs so formidably homely that it could have gone either way, and Munchkin lost, but she is a dog that should be commemorated.

Munchkin was a one-of-a-kind mutt that defied all species affili-ation. And she had fans.

Susie Lockheed, the owner of Sam, came back to the contest after his death with Tater Tot, who was Sam's longtime girlfriend and a mixture of Chihuahua and Chinese crested. Tater Tot was only 4.6 pounds and twice took home the trophy for ugliest mutt; Susie thought she might be just too cute to claim the big title.

Will Tater Tot follow Sam?

Grovie and Kaiya are two pugs from Santa Rosa owned by Edie and Jim Partridge. They attend the contest every year and represent the best of the good-natured fun the contest was intended to be. Their dogs often sport pug-friendly garb as they see themselves as ambassadors

The Partridge Family is pugnaciously attached to Pugs. Pictured here are Jim, Edie, Grovie, and Kaiya, all outfitted in their "pug ugly" T-shirts.

for a more pug-friendly world. Edie and Jim regularly attend the Butter & Egg Day Parade with a little wagon so the dogs can ride and wave (it's a full-body wriggle) at their adoring fans.

In 2006, Lucille Bald from Florida, Pee Wee Martini from Chicago, and Victoria from Southern California all came to lay claim to the title. Each was a fabulous specimen of dog and all were featured in the *People* magazine spread of dog and owner portraits shot by Mary Ellen Mark. Owned by Andrea Potts, Lucille Bald was an elegant Chinese crested with a thick pompadour, a neck of wrinkled skin, and a way of looking over her shoulder that was very commanding. Pee Wee Martini and his owner Kristin Maszkiewicz were a fashion match, each reflecting a punk-rock look that was amplified when they appeared together. Pee Wee was a Chinese crested/Japanese chin mix. If Pee Wee wasn't tattooed, he sure looked like it, but beyond that, his nose tilted to the side, and

Lucille Bald takes top honors in the Pedigree class in 2008.

Kristin and Pee Wee Martini bring punk elegance to the stage.

Victoria is used to the limelight.

his chin collapsed into his mouth where dangled the tongue. Victoria was an Italian greyhound with a pale blue sheen. Her smile, exhibited in photos and on stage, displayed a terrifying array of teeth. Her owner, Bruna Palmatier, rescued her and opened up a career of ugly-dog fame and glory.

Of special note in 2011 were another Lucille in the Mutt class and Cuda of the Pedigree class. Both had a wrestler's stance and in-your-face

Cuda and another Lucille, ready to wrestle.

Left: Handsome Hector and Ghada Marta. Right: Hector holds forth in his online blog and magazine. Below: Monkey debuts his monkey face.

attitude that were hilarious. Also returning was veteran Handsome Hector of the Pedigree class, who went on to blog to the masses about his experiences at the contest. Monkey too deserves some mention for both face and

73

name. Spam-o-Rama is a frequent entrant from Lydon Olivares, who started showing him four years ago when she was six years old and has returned every year since. Ashley Brown started with the contest as a teen and often her dogs, not as ugly as most, performed "stupid pet tricks" to win favor.

This page: Lydon Olivares, competing since age six, with Spam-o-Rama. Facing page: Ashley Brown's dogs may not be ugly, but they know some tricks.

Hosts & Judges

Hosts and judges add flavor to the show. The contest had run on radio personality Brent Farris's wit for more than a decade. But in 2010, the show started rotating emcees. The first was the 2007 *Last Comic Standing* winner Jon Reep, who delivered a show that was funny from start to finish. He was joined on stage by judges invited by that year's sponsor, House Of Dog, including Matt Scannell from the band

Left: Brent Farris emceed the World's Ugliest Dog Contest for more than a decade. Above: *Last Comic Standing* winner Jon Reep added his humor.

Vertical Horizon, television actress Christina Moore, and Karen "Doc" Halligan, a vet dedicated to animal welfare and pet-owner education who is also a television celebrity, appearing on *Animal Rescue 911, Dog Tales,* and *Dogs 101.* Halligan was returning from the previous year, when she shared the judges' table with Jon Provost ("Timmy" on the 1950s television show *Lassie*), and Brian Sobel, a fair board member. Sobel is the Randy Jackson of our show, providing continuity from year to year while educating the new judges on the

A line of celebrities made possible by sponsor House Of Dog in 2010.

Clockwise from top left: Christina Moore, winner Kathleen Francis, Matt Scannell, and Karen Halligan. In 2009, Pabst wins, surrounded by judges, host, and sponsors. Columnist Chris Smith returns to judge. Fair board member Brian Sobel is joined at the judging table by Jon Provost of *Lassie* fame and Doc Halligan. Jon Provost (aka Timmy) signs his book during the Dog Lover's Festival. Karen "Doc" Halligan made the perfect judge and also performed the vet checks.

process. Halligan also performed the vet checks for the contest for both years.

Many other judges have returned over the years, including Chris Smith from the *Santa Rosa Press Democrat* and local reporter Rayne Wolfe. There have also been stints from postal workers and county politicians. In 2011 local radio show hosts Rob and Joss of the country station *Froggy* double-teamed for a great show. The next year, the fair invited animal psychic Sonya Fitzpatrick to host, and in 2013, syndicated radio personalities Bob and Sheri hosted.

Radio personalities Rob and Joss from *Froggy* host in 2011.

Scandals & Controversy

There's much misbehavior that goes along with the World's Ugliest Dog Contest. Scandal erupted in 2006 when someone (who was never identified) gained unauthorized electronic access to the contest's Internet pre-voting page and deleted forty thousand votes from then leader Pee Wee Martini and thirty thousand votes from second-place Victoria. However, the winner of the World's Ugliest Dog Contest is not determined by the online voting. While it's a fun noncompetitive pre-event contest, allowing people to view the dogs and vote for their favorites, no prizes or glory really come with it. But it seemed that wasn't the view the hacker had. Although the fair webmaster Mike Gunn constructed some barriers, votes appeared rapidly, one every second on some of the contenders, while hundreds of votes continued to disappear from others.

Reports of the hacking swept the newspapers nationwide, with such headlines as "Ugly Dog Competition Gets Uglier," "Ugly Dogs Inspire Ugly Behavior by Humans." Someone was caring a bit too much,

Hackers mess with the online voting contest and cause a scandal.

Bring in the vets!

clearly. Finally, to rectify the situation, we had to completely restart Internet voting with e-mail recognition software in place. And every year since, we've had to watch it closely.

Astonishingly, there have been allegations by disgruntled contestants that the fair itself is a huge corporate conglomerate, making millions on the contest and using the contestants to achieve its nefarious aims. Please. We're a country fair, part of the state of California, with the aim of showcasing the best of our community and providing down-home entertainment. The contest runs on a minuscule budget with me, as the contest producer, its sole full-time employee for the weeks prior to the event. The winner claims a tall trophy, $1,000 from the fair, and the most valuable prize, a vault into fame. After the contest, rumors abound about the contest being fixed, the judges being biased, that I may be a secret breeder of Chinese cresteds and only want those dogs to win (my black lab gets testy when these accusations fly). These only underscore the depth of some contestants' desire to win. Ugly indeed.

There are always people who believe the dogs are getting their feelings hurt by being called ugly. It's obvious those folks had never been to the contest, or they would know that it is a celebration of dogs more than anything. But when Gus won the contest in 2008, there was talk. Was it right to associate a sick dog with the concept of ugly? What had always been a tongue-in-cheek spoof on dog shows suddenly became a bit tainted. With a sick

The fair instituted vet checks to ensure that all participants were healthy and naturally ugly.

dog winning, it suggested the possibility that if dogs were hurt or sick it might help them win—a ridiculous notion for fairs that have high standards for all animals and livestock shown. We only wanted dogs who were naturally ugly (or if you prefer, uniquely attributed) and we had the entire tradition of fairs behind us. In response, in addition to the usual vet papers that were required with registration, we instituted a vet check an hour before the contest, and any dog who did not pass was out. The Sonoma-Marin Fair also continued to partner with the Sonoma Humane Society to educate the public about animals and to provide opportunities to adopt rescue dogs. We brought it right into the contest with the popular "Beauty and the Beast Rescue Walks," where beauty queens walked adoptable dogs through the audience during the judging intervals of the show.

Media Mania

Until 2005, the media attending the World's Ugliest Dog Contest pretty much consisted of our three local newspapers. By 2006, it was a media frenzy.

Okay, now I'm going to drop a lot of names. Names like *Inside Edition, People* magazine, *Geraldo at Large,* Total Entertainment News, Incredible Features, Gannett Today, *Univision Network News,* Discovery Channel (Animal Planet), *PBS Foreign Exchange,* the Huffington Post, Yahoo, the Associated Press, ABC, NBC, CBS, Fox News, *The*

Newspapers around the world pick up the photo and story. Online media run with the announcement of the winner.

People magazine sends Mary Ellen Mark to shoot dog portraits.

Top left: Pre-event interviews.
Bottom left: Cameras jockey for position.
Center: The crowd is flanked by cameras.
Top right: Getting the perfect vantage point.
Bottom right: Interviews with the winner.

Waiting for the show.

Today Show, The Tonight Show, Good Morning America, Last Call with Carson Daly, Evening Magazine, The View with Barbara Walters, plus international film crews from Germany, Brazil, United Kingdom, Japan, and more. *People* magazine sent renowned photographer Mary Ellen Mark to do a photo shoot of the dogs and their owners. Animal Planet filmed the contest. Another forty-three million people saw the winner on the nightly news through television–affiliate broadcasts. And that was just in 2006. The World's Ugliest Dog Contest has put the town of Petaluma on a few maps.

For a small fair contest, this is a pretty big deal. But really, for any event, this is a huge deal.

Animal Planet

Animal Planet landed at the Sonoma-Marin Fair in 2006, 2008, and 2009, and what a difference a network makes. What passed for just another fun fair contest had to have some window dressing, and the World's Ugliest Dog Contest got a complete makeover courtesy of Animal Planet. Suddenly there were sets, including a large doghouse and a backdrop screen with white clouds for the stage and strategically placed planters. We even added a red carpet leading through the audience and up to the stage, so that contestants now walked through the audience rather

Animal Planet comes to Petaluma.

The crowds turn out for the Animal Planet taping of the show.

than appearing from above. The film crew followed dogs down the red carpet, up the stairs, and onto the platform, and a cameraman stayed on the stage to film the judging, with a giant boom camera over the top of the show. The excitement in the air was palpable and the audience was packed and exuberantly engaged. However, a juggernaut of other media was perturbed because they couldn't get the access they wanted now that Animal Planet's crew had taken command. The stupid pet tricks of past years were also out.

Animal Planet's host Debra Wilson Skelton joined our emcee Brent Farris on stage for the final announcement of the winner, and the network broadcast the segment nonstop for the year after

Top: Animal Planet's Debra Wilson Skelton hosts in 2006.
Bottom: The World's Ugliest Dog stage has a professional set.

The world's largest doghouse graces the stage as do the new tall trophies.

Beth Ostrosky hosts for Animal Planet in 2008.

the event. And the show gained even bigger name recognition and more media requests for passes. The following year, Animal Planet took a bye and continued to play segments from the year before. We embraced the changes and struck out on our own with sets, backdrop, front access, and holding pen for the contestants. In 2008, they returned to shoot the show again, this time with bigger and better sets. And Beth Ostrosky, a television personality and lover of animals, hosted with a great deal of grace and humor. They shot it one last time in 2009 for *Dogs 101,* and may return again in the future.

DOGumentary

The most in-depth rendering of the contest to date was done by filmmakers Don Lewis and John Beck in 2010. They'd both attended the contest for years as spectators and knew that even though it was all in good fun, there was quite a bit of below-the-surface tension and competition among the dog owners. After receiving permission from the fair, they followed some of the more colorful entrants—dogs *and* owners—for a few months leading up to and including the contest. The resulting hour-long documentary, *Worst in Show,* premiered in 2011. The film captures some of the rivalries between contestants but ultimately illustrates the good nature of the contest, shining a light on some of the more heart-rending stories, as well as the humor that is so central to the contest. The film toured the United States, including screenings in San Francisco and Petaluma, and won an award for

In 2010, filmmakers Don Lewis and John Beck shot *Worst in Show*.

The documentary film *Worst in Show* followed four contestants through the weeks leading up to and through the show. Clockwise, they were Jon Adler and Icky (pictured above and to right); Kathleen Francis and Princess Abby; Dane Andrew and Rascal; Ashley Brown and Winston (Winston shown here).

Best Documentary at the Kansas City International Film Festival before its world premiere on the Logo channel. It's now available online at worstinshowmovie.com.

Previously unseen shot of Sam playing it again.

Pabst gets candid for the camera.

Good Works & Fan Fair

Many of the entrants to the World's Ugliest Dog Contest are rescue dogs, and after the fair they go on to become ambassadors for the rescue dog movement. A big benefit to the world at large—directly due to this contest—is that many dogs get adopted in the name of ugly.

The fair itself encourages people to adopt rescue dogs at the contest via our Ugly Is the New Beautiful Fashion Show, featuring models and adoptable rescue dogs, and our Beauty and the Beast Rescue Walk, when local beauty queens parade adoptable rescue dogs from the Sonoma Humane Society through the crowd. The Humane Society has its Pet Waggin' parked at the event site all afternoon, so fairgoers can meet the animals available for adoption—and hopefully fall in love.

The Dog Lover's Festival is part of the pre-contest festivities to showcase dogs and the rescue movement.

Beauty and the Beast Rescue walks starring adoptable dogs and Sonoma County beauty queens.

Ugly is the New Beautiful Fashion Show featuring models from Julie Nation Academy in sponsor House Of Dog products refashioned as outfits. They walked adoptable dogs from the Sonoma Humane Society through the audience.

Judy Creel makes announcements throughout the day during the Dog Lover's Festival, which features dog presenters and tips on adopting.

On the stage on the afternoon of the show, we also hold the Dog Lover's Festival and bring in dog experts to talk about adoption, training, and feeding of dogs. And winners from the contest use their year of fame to spread the word about rescue dogs and how they make great pets. They are walking testimonials.

Many of the contestant owners have adopted rescue dogs. The Sonoma-Marin Fair provides that opportunity for the audience by hosting the Dog Lover's Festival preshow and inviting the Sonoma Humane Society to bring its Pet Waggin' with adoptable dogs.

Welcome to My World

The week of the World's Ugliest Dog Contest is a rush of preparation. Because the contest happens during the five-day fair, we don't actually get the chance to set up anything beforehand. The hypnotist works the stage until 11:00 the night before. So my job the morning of the contest is to direct the setup of the entire stage with the help of the fair crew as well as the grounds for the contest. That means erecting sets, signs, hauling in enormous doghouses and fire hydrants that are authentically heavy. It means setting up the media tent and the contestant check-in area. There are the tents for the vendors because starting at 1:00 p.m. with the opening of the fair, we're going to have the Dog Lover's Festival. (Who thought of that? Never mind, it seemed like a good idea months ago when we were brainstorming how to make everything bigger and better.) There's the red carpet that leads from the dog waiting area

through the audience and up to the stage. We need to construct the white picket fence around where the dogs and their owners will wait to be called (our holding pen). We've got to erect the thirty-foot signs over the entrance sign. Thank goodness we rehearsed the hosts the day before, unless of course they couldn't make it. Then we do it while the set goes up around us. It's an exercise in multitasking.

At 6:00 a.m. the day of the contest, there are media calling to see if they can get into the fair. Television crews want to bring in their vans, photographers want to set up a photo shoot, reporters want their interviews. I'm in a whirlwind of yes. I say yes to everyone and then somehow I have to make it happen. Luckily, I have the fair CEO Patricia Conklin to make it all work. Among many other things, she

The day of the event is a mad crush of setup and rehearsals in the morning, all of which must be completed in time for the opening of the Dog Lover's Festival at 1 p.m.

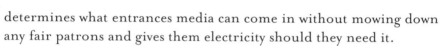

determines what entrances media can come in without mowing down any fair patrons and gives them electricity should they need it.

Miraculously, everything is ready, the fair opens, and folks start milling in. Fans, dogs, owners, media. By 3:00 p.m., it's reaching a fevered pitch. Ugly dogs have taken up their posts throughout the benches while members of the media conduct interviews, their large cameras poised to catch every bat of a doggie eyelash while their mics are thrust in the owner's face. This is where the veterans are separated from the newbies. The veterans have come ready to play, with an entourage of fans made up of family and friends garbed in T-shirts emblazoned with their dog's face and holding signs with the dog's name in bold letters. At this point, there seem to be more media than dogs, which makes for a kind of dash across the grass once a dog and his owner finish an interview. By 4:00 p.m., it's officially a

We check in each of the contestants to make sure they have turned in their registration forms and veterinarian documentation that the dog is in good health.

scene. Fans are starting to stake out their benches. Kids are starting to assemble on the lawn in front of the stage.

All the contestants join me for a brief mandatory meeting behind the stage. I lay it out for them. How they come in, where they walk, what they do once they get to the stage. I run through the contest, outlining the Pedigree, Mutt, runoff, and Ring of Champion rounds. If they are declared the winner, I let them know *The Today Show* is going to whisk them off to New York for a Sunday-morning interview. Then we give them their numbers and help them affix these to their chests (the owners, not the dogs). Then we direct them to the vet check booth where we have a vet ready to make sure their dog is healthy and eligible

As the producer, my day starts at 6 a.m. with phone interviews and requests for media access. Once at the fair, camera crews and reporters relentlessly document each of the contestants and interview the owners all afternoon before the contest begins at 6 p.m. Sometimes they even manage to capture me mid-sprint.

The mandatory meeting for contestants backstage is where we give owners instructions on where to be when and answer any questions. Media grab shots here too.

Vet checks are performed to verify that the contestants are healthy and can compete. The duties are performed by qualified vets. Pictured here at left: Petaluma's Central Animal Pet Hospital vet Matthew Carter. For two years, television personality and vet Karen "Doc" Halligan did the honors.

Contestants take the red carpet to the holding pen before the show starts.

Contestants wait nervously in the holding pen for the show to begin.

to compete. Once we're back in front of the stage, the media will document the vet checks, but before then, the vet and I confer about who is not going to make the cut. I have to give that owner and dog the sad news. I adjust the host's script to reflect the change. It's getting close. Almost time for the contest.

There's a big crush now for any available space on the grass in front of the stage. Media have started working their way into the corners of the stage area, a few creeping up onto the stage, until I send them down again. I'm walking through the crowd to clear the red carpet for the 5:30 Red Carpet Walk, in which we bring all of the contestants into the holding pen. Drumroll please! The owners parade in numerical order through the audience and into the holding pen. The crowd is buzzing, media are inching back to the space I just kicked them out of, the judges are assembling behind the stage. I whip back there to meet with them and give them the judging slips. I leave them in the capable hands of Brian Sobel, veteran judge and fair board member. And then the show starts.

The Show

After so much preparation, it's finally time for the contest. The show is scheduled for sixty minutes, which is an epic commitment of time in the fast-paced, distracted air of a country fair. Often it runs over, yet people stay through the whole thing—*and* it's a show that people return to each year. We have our volunteer judges poised to make their determination, but the audience gets a vocal say in the final choice by cheering loudly for their favorites. First there's the Pedigree round with a winner selected from the contestants. Then there's the Mutt round with another winner selected. Then there's a runoff between the Pedigree and the Mutt winner. But no, the last dog standing is *not* the World's Ugliest Dog. There's a final runoff in what we call the Ring of Champions, where the winner of the Pedigree/Mutt challenge for the current year goes up against all the past winners of the World's Ugliest Dog Contest! Here's how it looks from the audience.

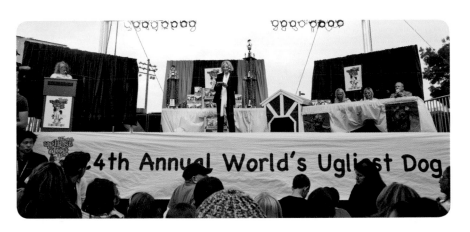

Facing page:
Audience politicking
continues throughout
the show.
Left: I confer with the
film crew from the UK
about red carpet shots.
Below: Kids gather in
front of the stage.

Let's bring out the contestants!

Appeals are made to

the host,

the judges,

and the audience.

The hosts ask questions and chat it up with the audience while dogs wait patiently.
(You know they are thinking, "Bring on the chicken strips!")

Time to bring all the contestants back on stage.

The audience may text in their votes a la *American Idol* or folks may shout out their choice.

Meanwhile, the dogs think their thoughts, "Nap or chicken strips? Chicken strips or nap?"

"I vote
nap."

Two winners, Princess Abby and Yoda, reflect on what it all means.

And winners are declared! Shots from the final moments of several years' contests follow. Below: Beth Ostrosky with 2008 winner Gus and owners. Right and bottom: Posing with Rascal, one of the Ring of Champions, and during the final round in which Gus is named the World's Ugliest Dog.

The 2009 runoff between the winner of the Pedigree class, Miss Ellie, and the winner of the Mutt class, Pabst.

Pabst beats out the Ring of Champions to win it all.

The 2012 Ring of Champions round results in the UK's Mugly beating past winners Princess Abby and Rascal to win it all.

After the Show

After the World's Ugliest Dog is declared, madness ensues. Every camera is trained on the winning dog and the stage is rushed with media and well-wishers. I'm not much help in managing the onslaught, as I need to hustle back to my office to e-mail the photo of the winner along with the official press release to media outlets around the world. I also field media questions via phone and e-mail, and prepare a video of the declaration, which we post on YouTube within hours of the contest conclusion. This goes viral over the weekend, and remains for perpetuity on our own website, www.sonoma-marinfair.org.

The winners from each of the Pedigree and Mutt classes eventually come into the office and we arrange for their winnings. We cut the big check to the winner. At about 11:00 p.m., it's over for this year's contest, but for the winning dog, it's just beginning.

Mugly and Bev are whisked away in a limo to the Sheraton Sonoma County in Petaluma for a dog-friendly dinner and overnight stay. After that, they'll field media interviews from around the world.

A Bit of History

While 2013 marks the 25th anniversary of the Sonoma-Marin Fair running the contest, it actually started in the 1970s as part of the Old Adobe Festival. Sonoma-Marin took it on as part of their annual five-day fair in 1988.

In the first few decades at the fair, the contest had lots of elements. Brent Farris, who emceed the contest for many of the shows, had an audience-inclusive style that involved his telling a series of jokes about ugly dogs ("that dog is so ugly he has to sneak up on his water

No Bones About It — He's the Ugliest Dog

Shocker! Mexican Cops & Politicians Are Driving Stolen American Cars

bowl"—you get the idea). It was very much a relaxed kind of contest with people walking across the stage or meandering off mid-show. It always drew a big crowd, but with a small number of contestants, and the whole thing wrapped up in forty-five minutes, including Stupid Pet Tricks. There were local dignitaries as judges and a lot of standing around waiting for winners to be announced.

One of our regular contestants, Dane Andrew, started competing in the World's Ugliest Dog Contest back in 1977 when he was eleven years old. We have him to thank for being our historian and supplying photos from the old days.

Dane took the title with Chi Chi (left) starting the dynasty of eight wins, and landing in *Guinness World Records*. Lady Pink (below left) and Mai Tai (right) each won three times. Rascal (below right), son of Mai Tai, poses with his trophies.

Clockwise from top left: Lily Tomlin and Alan Alda strike the pose. Amanda Bynes loves Rascal. *Happy Days*! Barbara Walters will get to the bottom of it. Adam West gives Rascal the nickname Bat-Dog.

Celebrity Status

True, Lassie is more famous, as is Rin Tin Tin, but it's possible that World's Ugliest Dog winner Rascal has shaken more paws. He has his Acting Guild card (as does his owner Dane Andrew), and is on the short list when casting directors are working on horror and campy films. Wonder who was Zombie Dog in the movie *Tele-Zombie*? Rascal, of course. Coming soon are appearances in the movie *Curse of the Smoke O'Lantern* and *The Adventures of Skany Doo*, a short film that will air in schools and children's film festivals to raise money and awareness for animal rescue. Rascal has also been featured in more than twenty television shows, and together Dane and Rascal have a star on the Palm Springs Walk of Fame. That's what the title of World's Ugliest Dog can do for you. Here are some of the stars that they've met.

Above: Who's funny now, Kevin Nealon?

Below: Rascal on *Last Call with Carson Daly*.

Rascal does the celebrity circuit. Clockwise from top left: Anne Rice or Rascal, who tells the more terrifying "tail"? Rascal meets Jane Russell. George Lopez shares his star power. Lou Diamond Phillips and Dane do ties while Rascal does leopard. Carol Channing says, "You're looking swell, Rascal." Jay Leno introduces the world-famous Rascal.

Pamela Anderson does a beauty inspection. Pit Boss Shorty and the dogs. Dr. Phil prescribes a makeover. Ashley Judd. Rascal brings out the animal in Jenny McCarthy. Bonnie Raitt poses in the early days of the contest with Dane Andrew, his mother, Doris Birkland Beezley, and dogs Mai Tai and Rascal (held by Dane). Donald Trump and Rascal share the spotlight.

Mugs in the Online Voting Gallery

One of the things that is most obvious about the owners of ugly dogs is that they love their animals, have bigger hearts than most, and have a devastating sense of humor. These are the bios submitted by the owners for the World's Ugliest Dog Contest online voting gallery, which precedes the contest each April and gives the public a chance to view the contestants. No prizes are awarded for the winner of the online contest, but nonetheless it's a source of great pride to win. In fact, past online voting contests have been hacked and results tampered with. But we chuckle, throw up a few obstacles to prevent cheating, and reset the contest votes to zero and shoulder on. Here are the written appeals made by the owners for online votes from the last several years.

Chopper

❝❝Hi, Ugly Dog Lover! I won 1st place in 2010 for World's Ugliest Mutt. Watch out ugly dogs; see you soon. I am older, smarter, and still ugly!❞❞

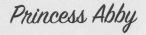

Princess Abby

"Princess Abby is a rescue dog who saved her owner's life by coming into it at just the right time. Adorable as she is to her owner, Abby is missing an eye (probably from birth), and hunches over because her front legs are shorter than her back legs (a possible result of inbreeding). Found on the streets near death, she was taken in, given a new loving home, and nursed back to health, and now she never wants to venture far from her owner. She swept every division at the 2010 World's Ugliest Dog Contest and took the top prize to the surprise of her owner. From there, life got even better. She boarded a plane for an appearance on *The Today Show!* Princess Abby starred in the documentary, *Worst in Show.* And sporting new outfits—designed just for her—Princess Abby has been an ambassador for helping rescue dogs wherever she appears."

Rascal

❝❝Rascal is the original 2002 World's Ugliest Dog winner and "Ring of Champions" titleholder who is ready to come back and challenge the ugliest of the ugly. Owned by actor Dane Andrew of Sunnyvale, California, Rascal is a naturally hairless, never shaven, seven pound crazy critter, complete with Einstein hair, crooked face, and a tongue that hangs out due to being born without many teeth. Rascal is from an ugly dog dynasty, with his rescue grandfather, Chi Chi, in *Guinness World Records* for winning seven world titles, and even his grandmother, Lady Pink, and mother, Mai Tai, won three titles themselves. Rascal is so ugly that he has done a few horror films that are coming out soon, and has a cartoon strip and documentary on the way, both named *The Ugliest Dog*. Rascal uses his ugly for good with fund-raisers and soon a patented trademark hot dog leash, to help give back to the animal kingdom with a percentage of proceeds donated to animal charities. To us, Rascal is the most handsome being to ever live and is a loving family member, but it's in fun when he is called ugly, so please consider Rascal as your favorite ugly.❞❞

Rue

"Watch out folks, Rue is coming back! She is a year older and wiser and five pounds heavier. Her head has not grown but her body looks like a sausage, and her mullet . . . well, it is more fabulous than ever, and some say she looks like a rat, a warthog, or something from the wild. People often stop and stare when they drive by our home. She is by far the strangest dog we have ever had, and if you want to know why, you'll have to come to Petaluma to meet her!"

Squiggy

"Squiggy is a rescue dog and is five years old. He's a goofy-looking character with a sky-high, spikey Mohawk, chicken legs, and a tongue that is always hanging out of his mouth. (We say that he's aesthetically challenged.) He prefers the couch to a walk in the park any day. We are often stopped by folks asking to take a photo of him, since it is not very often you see a dog like Squig (and the fact is that he's quite photogenic). He's a mix of Chinese crested, Japanese chin, a hint of gremlin, and a dash of Smurf. I know that he'd appreciate your vote—really."

Hercules the Pug

"I am fourteen years old. I have lost an eye several years ago due to cataracts. I am blind with cataracts in my other eye. My mom says my nose is dry and looks like a mushroom. I am Mom's first and only failure as a foster parent. I am very happy sleeping all day on my beanbag and pillow and going for long walks in my stroller. I have nothing to complain about even though I cannot see or walk well anymore. It is okay to say that I am not perfect or beautiful in the traditional sense, so please vote for me as the ugliest dog. Thank you."

Icky

"Icky is a rescue from Butte County who resides in his forever home in Davis, California. At just two years old, he has seen his share and done his part. Icky never passes up the opportunity to raise money for local nonprofits that are desperately in need. This marks the third World's Ugliest Dog Contest for this handsome man. And one thing is sure: Icky can't wait to see you all at the fair."

Harley

"Hi, I'm Harley. I'm a rescue dog, about two years old. My new family picked me from a bunch of other dogs at a rescue in Lodi, California. Someone dumped me at a shelter with a broken leg and now I'm awesome, thanks to my new owners. Everywhere I go people are always asking my mom and dad what I am. I don't really know what I am, but my mom says I look like half possum and half billy goat! I won the ugliest dog in Fort Bragg, California, during Paul Bunyan Days. It was pretty exciting! Maybe they'll take me to the World's Ugliest Dog Contest one day."

Creature

"Creature is a ten-year-old Mexican hairless mix. We rescued her last year from a local shelter in Utah. She resided there for over a month with no one expressing any interest in her until we came along. Creature recently won the title of "Utah's Ugliest Mutt." She is the kindest dog we have ever met. She weighs forty-one pounds and is mostly hairless, except for her long blonde hair on her head and tail. She helps promote our private dog rescue, RSQ DOGS, with her unique smile!"

Handsome Hector

"It ain't pretty being UGLY. . . . Just when we thought that being good-looking was the end-all to a "happy" life, Handsome Hector has singlehandedly shown through his ravishing exterior that beauty is not only skin deep but that anyone can obtain love and the "high life" in spite of a hideous exterior. Born in Sacramento (circa 2000) with the heart and mannerisms of a true junkyard dog, Handsome Hector, aka Hecki, is, in his own opinion, devastatingly handsome. He is short (approximately three inches off the ground), fat, bald, and never misses a day to alarm the general public with his handsomeness. He's quite proud and confident of his two combed hairs, and his confidence renders him fearless! Farting, snorting, and smearing his naked body with duck excrement are just a few of the talents acquired during his time spent in finishing school. Despite all efforts on his mother's part to refine him, he continues to go where no other scrapper can or is willing to go . . . garbage cans, alleyways, public toilets, and junkyards, searching for that one divine crumb. Handsome Hector's life motto is to eat like a pig, look like a rat, and lounge like a bloated seal! http://handsome-hector.blogspot .com. **"**

Monkey

❝Can this really be a dog? Monkey is a one-year-old Chinese crested/Brussels griffon mix. This will be her second year in the contest. She was rescued from a hoarding situation and found a loving home with a family who think she is the cutest thing, in her own way. She has long, hairless, model-like legs and has no fear of anything, especially the competition. She is a very happy dog who enjoys going to the dog park, where she is always the talk of the park. She is a very outgoing little dog who gets along with every dog, cat, or person she comes in contact with. Please remember, when you go to adopt a dog, fluffy and cute are everywhere. It takes a special dog to be ugly.❞

Aboo

❝When he was born, we called Isaboo's litter the "Boo Babies." He is a Boo too, hence the name. His hair often flips over to the side and looks just like a Donald Trump comb-over! If that doesn't say "UGLY," what does? He has the sweetest personality and is always so happy to see his people. This picture was taken when he just woke up. I promise he is actually a very pretty boy!❞

Mugly

"Eight-year-old Mugly is a Chinese crested and a rescue dog. Mugly has had hard times and was viciously attacked in a park by a group of thugs a couple of years ago. He's now a Pets as Therapy dog, working with children. In addition, he raises money for rescue charities by holding online dog pageants and competitions. His lovely personality outweighs his looks, and people love him wherever he goes."

Peeps

"Peeps, aka Little Bo Peep, came into my life two years ago after being rescued late one night from a Missouri puppy mill. Weighing five pounds and in excruciating pain with an eye ready to rupture from advanced glaucoma, she arrived in Alabama looking like a raw chicken with no personality. Her eye was immediately removed. She is blind in the remaining eye. In just a few weeks she began to blossom. She is now a thirteen-pound, nine-year-old lady full of grace! Peeps is also the star in an upcoming movie to be released in 2013."

Reggie

"Reggie is quite a dog. He has a personality that's hard to put your finger on and a face to match. What can we tell you? Well Reggie loves everyone and everything, so keep your mouth closed when you first meet him as he is prone to giving unwanted tongue kisses. Reggie likes to chase things and since so many of the people and animals who meet him run away, this works out well. Reggie's hair grows, or doesn't grow, in so many places we're not sure whether to shave him or treat him with Rogaine. We tried tossing a coin but Reggie ate it. So now when people say Reggie's priceless we say, "Nope, he's worth about twenty-five cents." We wondered, if we looked up "unusual" in the dictionary, would Reggie's picture be next to it? Unfortunately, no. We weren't able to find him until we looked up "Good God, is that a dog?" and there he was. And so here he is, and he wants you to vote for him as the ugliest dog in the world."

Pabst

"This is Pabst, the 2009 Champion! Pabst has had a quiet year off, but still enjoys the attention his underbite brings and is looking to take back the crown of World's Ugliest! This will more than likely be Pabst's final year of entering the contest. He will retire and spend the rest of his life sunbathing and playing tug-of-war with his sister Corky."

Grovie Partridge

"Grovie is an eight-year-old male pug,
This is the third contest for the lug.
Yes, he has many rolls about his face,
A judge could disappear in there without a trace!

He snores, farts, and sits like a frog,
His legs hang off the couch, he's a bump on a log!
Chews on Mom's hair,
Sneezes and sprays boogers in the air.

He loves to sneak cat food every chance he gets,
His dad Jim repeatedly says, "Get outta there!" and frets.
But his memory is short, with a stomach never full,
Off again smooshing food with his face in the bowl!

In his pic he looks like a *Star Wars* Ewok,
When people see him at the fair they come by and talk,
Saying, "He's a pug, he's not ugly!"
Even though he is wrinkly and his eyes are bugly.

His sister Kaiya was once in the group,
Like him, competing in the ugly-dog troupe.
Come see us on June twenty-four,
Cheer your favorite dog with a scream, yell, or roar!"

Pee Wee Martini

"Peewee Martini is a six-year-old Chinese crested/Japanese chin mix from Philadelphia, Pennsylvania. This healthy little mutt's crooked face says it all! I'm ugly and cuddly and oh so snuggly!"

Cuda

"Cuda was born deformed. Her back legs are weak and shorter than her front legs. She has a curved spine and her shoulders jut forward and her neck has some limited movement. She has a severe underbite and snorts like a pig. Even her front legs are not the same length and her feet are flat! Her tail doesn't even look like it's attached correctly and her ears face different ways . . . her face is smooshed, too! Yet, she is the kindest and gentlest dog ever and has been given a clean bill of health by the vet. She is not in pain but who knows if at some point in her life her hips will develop problems. That's why I want her to have the opportunity to show the world that even deformed dogs are beautiful. We believe she is a mix between a pit bull and a gargoyle!"

Kaiya

❝Kaiya is a ten-year-old female pug,
This is her second time showing her mug!
She looks like a cross between a seal and Jabba the Hut,
Her neck rolls aren't indicative of her gut!

She actually is a trim little girl,
Come to the Ugly Dog Contest and give her a twirl.
But after Doc Halligan's once-over a few years back,
She said, "She could shed a few pounds," to be exact.

She enjoys participating in all the festivities in the contest,
Hanging out with her dog buds and looking her ugly best!
Walking the red carpet to the stage,
Photographed, interviewed, and checked out by the judges
is quite the rage.

This year her brother Grovie will be in the mix,
Strutting his stuff while photographers take many pics.
Come check us out June 24th at the Petaluma Fair,
See the ugly dogs in all their flair.❞

Ratdog

❝Ratdog is a fourteen-year-old deaf rescue
mutt who eats onions, garlic, and anchovies on his
pizza.❞

Yoshi

I'm Yoshi! I am a Wonder Dog. I got rescued by the wonderful people at Wonder Dog Rescue in 2010. Just prior to this I had been picked up by animal control with a severe case of dermodex. Obviously, I have had some surgery on my back leg and I'm missing a toe off that foot. My front legs are a bit deformed. I'm not quite sure if this is a birth defect or the result of malnutrition or injury. My vet says as my legs are functioning and I'm getting around fine, so it's probably best not to mess with them further right now. My lower front teeth are worn with one tooth missing so my tongue often sticks out of my mouth and my bat ears are chewed and scarred from mange mites. Because my front legs are shorter than my hind legs my bum end rides a bit higher than my front end. This makes for my funny profile. I also have a rather peculiar fat neck that gathers into wrinkles and a disproportionately broad chest. I'm not quite sure of my origins as I am a rescue dog, but I may be a purebred Boston bull terrier. Some people think I may be a French bulldog and Boston terrier mix. I am participating in the World's Ugliest Dog Contest because I know it will be great fun and will promote awareness of the great dogs people can adopt from animal shelters and rescue groups. I hope you will consider me for your pick as the World's Ugliest Dog!

Spam-o-Rama

Spam-o-Rama is a caricature of the school nerd with the confidence to ask out the head cheerleader . . . and get a date! He may be wearing a day-glo rain jacket and have ophthalmic ointment in both eyes, but he thinks he's a rock star. He's not concerned that he has thin patches of platinum hair or perhaps six teeth in his head. When not being bossed by Reggie the rooster, Spammy lives a life of luxury with his lady, a harlequin Great Dane. She has enough body heat for them both and always saves him spooning space on her beds . . . yes, beds.

An overbred Chinese crested, Spam-o-Rama will be competing in his third World's Ugliest Dog competition. On the way home from his first competition, after not placing, Spam's confidence was restored when a man lounging on his motorcycle gasped, "That's the ugliest dog in the world!" In fact, Spam was not the World's Ugliest Dog—Pabst was. But Spam vowed to return.

Spam-o-Rama really has unfortunate aesthetics. His dry, crusty nose looks like it may chip off at any time. His tear ducts were removed in a surgery to repair eyelids that were turning inside out, thus the constant ointment and partial blindness. He has a dreadlock on his back from the ceaseless fashions he's forced to endure. (He'd scratch himself up from allergies otherwise.) The clothing also facilitates the doggie-farmer tan, for which Spam-o-Rama is famous. And the bumps and pimples, ugh.

How did we end up with the chupacabra dog? Several years ago, our vet told us of an elderly couple who needed to rehome their two Chinese cresteds. The dogs were always under foot and were a safety hazard to the couple. We agreed to foster the dogs until we could find loving, forever homes for them. (You know this part, right?)

Spam-o-Rama looks forward to dazzling you with his regrettable appearance and magnetic charm. Don't look into his eyes when he asks you for a date! "

Sputnick

" Sputnick loves everybody! Sputnick is a two-year-old Brussels griffon. He loves cats, birds, and people (adults and children). Sputnick is a therapy dog and goes to work at an outpatient drug rehab where he gives affection to clients. He also watches out for my father with dementia and waits at the end of the driveway for his bus to arrive every weekday from his day program. It just goes to show, beauty is only skin deep! Many people think he is straight out of *Star Wars*. Who do you think he looks like? "

Lucille

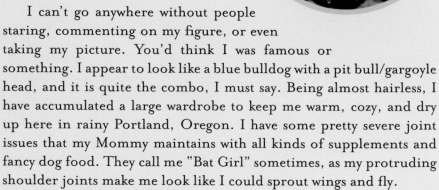

"My name is Lucille, but I go by Lucy, unless I'm in trouble.

I was rescued from a high-kill shelter in Los Angeles and adopted by my forever family last year. The nice lady who rescued me never thought I'd find a home as I have a few issues . . . but who doesn't?

I can't go anywhere without people staring, commenting on my figure, or even taking my picture. You'd think I was famous or something. I appear to look like a blue bulldog with a pit bull/gargoyle head, and it is quite the combo, I must say. Being almost hairless, I have accumulated a large wardrobe to keep me warm, cozy, and dry up here in rainy Portland, Oregon. I have some pretty severe joint issues that my Mommy maintains with all kinds of supplements and fancy dog food. They call me "Bat Girl" sometimes, as my protruding shoulder joints make me look like I could sprout wings and fly.

Emotionally I am doing much better now, thanks to my Prozac. When I get stressed or just don't know what to do with myself I spin and spin and spin! Then I try to eat the furniture. I'm not trustworthy in the car as I have eaten a seatbelt or two. I don't know why I do it and with these pit-bull jaws, I can really chew. Sometimes people think I look scary but I love everyone I meet and everyone who meets me loves me too, but they all end up saying, "Something's just not quite right with her."

I don't care because my family loves me even with all my issues.

I flunked out of doggy day care—just too much stimulation for me, aka lots of spinning, so my family got me my own dog pack and adopted me a brother and a sister. Yeehaw!

I'm surprisingly fast for my shape and love to chase squirrels, birds, and cats—in fact anything that will run from me. When I'm not running I am asleep on the couch waiting to roll over for anyone to come by and give me a good belly rub.

This is my first time in the Ugly Dog Contest. I'm a bit nervous but would love your support. "

Elvis

"Elvis is a Chinese Crested/minpin mix. He is an odd little fellow with a crazy personality. His favorite thing to do is stand on his head! He was rescued from a hoarder and now lives the good life with several other rescue dogs. He likes to go to schools to teach kids pet responsibility and bite prevention. He is also an advocate for rescue dogs! When people see his hairdo they think Elvis, or Eddie Munster! It looks like a toupee! He has three goals in life: to eat, sleep, and be on *Ellen* (he would love to stand on his head and look up at her!). He has a Facebook fan page under Comedy Barn Canines. Check him out along with his other canine pals! "

Thanks

Although I'm not sure about my tombstone reading "World's Ugliest Dog Contest Producer," I'm proud to be in on the worldwide phenomenon that comes with the role. I may never visit China, but that doesn't mean they haven't run the photo of the winner like hundreds of other countries around the world. I get to participate in a small but singular bit of humor that strikes the world's funny bone.

There are lots of people who make the World's Ugliest Dog Contest happen, not the least of which is the Sonoma-Marin Fair staff, board, and volunteers. Especially worthy of praise for logistical feats of last-minute variations is CEO Patricia Conklin. Pat is great as a sounding board and problem solver when listening to the venting that naturally arises in coordinating such a monumental event. (I'm trying to say thanks for being there for the meltdowns.) Also credit goes to staffers Cara Parlata and Rich Gravelle, and newly retired Nis Peterson and his crew. I appreciate the work of webmaster Mike Gunn, who fought the hacking of our online voting gallery with his good and creative nature. Thanks to Judy Creel for handling the stage on the big day like a pro. Brian Sobel, judge and contest steward, deserves thanks as well for always thinking of the big picture and listening better than most anyone else, Thanks, too, to all the judges who volunteer their time, especially Chris Smith and Rayne Wolfe who often jump in at the last minute. Also to my dear friends who sense when I'm overwhelmed and come rushing in to help, especially on the day of the contest: Amy Appleton, Cheryl Fink, Michelle Murphy, and Carolyn Rasmussen.

Special thanks go to the photographers who shoot the contest each year for free or for next to nothing in exchange for being part of it. Kira Stackhouse of Nuena Photography has been the official photographer for the World's Ugliest Dog Contest for the last three years, always getting me the shot minutes after the contest so we can send it around the world. Grace Chon of Shine Pet Photos volunteered as the official photographer the two years prior to that and captured many great moments. Both Brett Klenk and Scott Hess shot a year of the contest while doing the rest of the fair as well and delivered some fantastic photos. I'd also like to thank Dane Andrew for supplying information and access to historical photos and to him and Yvonne Morones both for filling in gaps I had in knowledge. Thanks, too, to the videographers over the years who kick out videos after the contest that always go viral on YouTube (Bob Kennedy, Thomas Harrigan, and Alan Fitch).

Thanks to the media who cover this contest each year. It's a highly visual story and you've translated it well for millions to enjoy.

Thanks to the dog owners and your wonderful dogs whom I've come to know over the years and those I've yet to meet.

I appreciate Agent Andy Ross for thinking that the world could use an ugly-dog chuckle year-round in the form of this book, and to Lyons Press for agreeing. Writing encouragement came from Sue Olsen McCullough and the Morgan clan.

Lastly, thanks to the crew at home who tolerate the hysteria every year: Mitch, Britt, Taylor, Alex, and the family dog, Chloe.

Photo Credits

KIRA STACKHOUSE / NUENA.COM
Pages i, iv (top right), 2 (left), v3, 4 (top left, bottom left), 7 (both), 8–9, 11 (inset), 12, 13 (center), 19 (bottom), 22 (top right; bottom), 25, 27, 32 (top), 33, 52, 57–62, 64–67, 70 (center left; bottom left, bottom right), 72 (bottom), 73 (top left; bottom), 79 (center), 80, 82, 87 (bottom), 88, 95 (bottom right), 98 (top left; bottom left) 101 (right), 102 (left), 103 (right), 104–105 (center), 105 (top right; bottom right), 106 (top left), 107, 109, 111–113, 114 (top left; bottom right), 115, 116 (top right; center right; bottom), 117–118, 122, 126–129, 136–137, 139 (top), 140–146, 147 (bottom), 148–152

GRACE CHON / SHINE PET PHOTOS
Pages 5, 6, 17, 24 (right), 26 (left), 41 (right), 50 (left), 51 (right), 53–54, 55 (top), 56, 76 (right), 77, 78 (top left), 78–79 (top center; bottom center, bottom right), 83, 86 (top), 95 (middle left; bottom left), 97, 100 (left), 100–101 (center), 102–103 (center), 104 (top left; bottom left), 106 (top right), 108, 110, 116 (top left), 119 (full page)

SCOTT HESS / SCOTTHESSPHOTO.COM
Pages iii, iv (bottom), 4 (center left, bottom left, bottom right), 11 (full page), 13 (top; bottom left), 14–15, 18, 19 (top), 22 (top left), 23, 24 (left), 26 (right), 41 (left), 42, 43 (top), 44–49, 50–51 (center), 68, 74–75, 76 (left), 78 (bottom left), 93, 98 (top right), 99, 106 (bottom), 114 (top right; bottom left), 121, 123–125

BRETT KLENK / BCKPHOTOGRAPHY.COM
Pages 2 (right), 16, 20–21, 37 (full page), 38–40, 43 (bottom), 69 (center; bottom), 70 (top right), 71, 72 (top), 86 (bottom), 86–87 (center), 87 (top), 89–92, 120, 147 (top)

MANY THANKS TO THE OTHERS WHO HAVE PROVIDED PHOTOS:
Sonoma-Marin Fair: page iv (top left)
Dane Andrew: pages 31, 32 (bottom), 130–135, 138
Susie Lockheed: pages 34, 36, 37 (inset), 96 (top)
Yvonne Morones: pages 28–30, 69 (top)
Ghada Marta: page 73 (top right)
John Beck and Don Lewis from the documentary *Worst in Show*: pages 55 (bottom), 94, 95 (top left), 96 (bottom)
Jeffrey Werner: page 35